Confession

God Gives Us Truth

The Lutheran Spirituality Series

John T. Pless

CONCORDIA PUBLISHING HOUSE · SAINT LOUIS

Copyright © 2006 Concordia Publishing House
3558 S. Jefferson Ave., St. Louis, MO 63118-3968
1-800-325-3040 • www.cph.org

Written by John T. Pless

Edited by Robert C. Baker

This publication may be available in braille, in large print, or on cassette tape for the visually impaired. Please allow 8 to 12 weeks for delivery. Write to Lutheran Blind Mission, 7550 Watson Rd., St. Louis, MO 63119-4409; call toll-free 1-888-215-2455; or visit the Web site: www.blindmission.org.

Manufactured in the United States of America

1 2 3 4 5 6 7 8 9 10 15 14 13 12 11 10 09 08 07 06

Contents

Hymnal Key

LSB=Lutheran Service Book
ELH=Evangelical Lutheran Hymnary
CW=Christian Worship
LW=Lutheran Worship
LBW=Lutheran Book of Worship
TLH=The Lutheran Hymnal

About This Series

In the West, spirituality is as nebulous as it is popular. Having succumbed to humanism, rationalism, and Darwinism, communities once known for a genuine Christian piety now provide a fertile breeding ground for self-made theologies, Eastern religions, the worship of science and technology, or even a resuscitation of the old pagan gods. In a highly competitive environment, each of these spiritual philosophies seeks to fill the vacuum left by the seemingly departed Christian spirit.

Even among faithful Christians, and at other times and places, spirituality has run the gamut from the mystical to the almost sterile. From the emotional to the pragmatic, the experiential to the cerebral, the all-too-human desire to experience (and control!) the divine has proven to be especially resilient. Influenced by modernism, postmodernism, and whatever comes next, even those who try faithfully to follow Jesus Christ may find defining *spirituality*, or at least what is distinctively Christian about their own beliefs and practices, a significant challenge.

Do Lutheran Christians have a spirituality? Indeed they do! This adult Bible study series explores the rich depths of a distinctively Lutheran spirituality that begins in Baptism and is founded upon God's Word. There, the incarnate, crucified, and resurrected Lord proclaims His victory over sin, death, and the devil, and from there flows the proclamation of His Gospel and the administration of His Sacraments. It is through these means presented within the liturgy of His Church that Christ communicates not merely spiritual energies, an emotional high, a method of reasoning, or a stringent morality, but truly Himself—God in human flesh.

Written by respected Lutheran scholars in the United States and Australia, this adult Bible study series emphasizes the Bible, Luther's catechism, and the Lutheran hymnal as concrete and integral resources for a truly Lutheran spirituality. May God richly bless those who study His Word, and through His Word may they experience the genuinely enlightening and life-giving spirituality found only in the life, death, and resurrection of our Lord and Savior, Jesus Christ.

The Editor

Participant Introduction

In the memorable words of the sixth chief part of Luther's Small Catechism, "where there is the forgiveness of sins there is also life and salvation." Lutheran spirituality has as its heart the forgiveness of sins. In contrast to competing forms of spirituality that might be characterized by moral improvement, celebration of the divine presence, or growth toward holiness, Lutheran spirituality is always a return to the baseline of the forgiveness of sins. The Absolution, spoken in liturgy and sermon and given with the body and blood of Jesus in the Lord's Supper, moves us back into the world where we live in our various callings. It is precisely in those callings that the continued reality of our sinfulness is made manifest. We fail to fear, love, and trust in God above all things and thus we do not love our neighbors as ourselves. We are continually driven back to Jesus, to confess our sins and receive what only His blood can impart, forgiveness of sins, which carries with it both pardon and the power for the new life.

Forgiveness of sins is only for sinners. Those who do not see themselves as sinners will find this topic irrelevant at best and offensive at worst. But if you know yourself to be a real sinner who lives only by the promise of the Absolution, keep on reading. This is not a study about how one might feel about his or her sins. It is not a handbook that will provide you with a few easy techniques to master those bad habits that make your life and the lives of those around you a misery. This little volume is an exploration of truth. It is a study of the truth of your sin in the eyes of God. In this study, we hear the truth that comes out of His mouth in the Word of the Law that convicts and kills you. Agreement with that truth is called confession. But our study cannot end there, for there is an ultimate Word of truth about sinners that comes from the mouth of God. It is called Absolution. The Word of the Gospel in all of its various forms—spoken, sacramental, written, or remembered—is nothing less than an Absolution; God's own verdict that the sinner will not die but live by trust in the promise.

This study will probe Confession and Absolution in the multiple ways that they are given us, such as the Lord's Prayer, the Divine Service, words of repentance and forgiveness spoken between brothers and sisters in Christ Jesus, and that often overlooked and underused gift of our heritage, individual Confession and Absolution before one's pastor. The goal of this study is to deepen in you the knowledge of Absolution as the comfort and consolation that Christ alone provides when the devil terrorizes you, tempting you to believe his lie that there is no forgiveness of your sins.

For those of you who wish to supplement this study, I would recommend the following books that I have found helpful: Oswald Bayer, *Living by Faith: Justification and Sanctification* (Eerdmans), Gerhard Forde, *On Being a Theologian of the Cross* (Eerdmans), Henry Hamann, *On Being a Christian* (Northwestern), Herman Preus, *A Theology to Live By* (CPH), and Harold Senkbeil, *Dying to Live: The Power of Forgiveness* (CPH). Each of these authors in his own way has helped me better understand confession and forgiveness of sin and their insights are often reflected in this short book.

To prepare for "The Truth of Sin," read 1 John 1:8–10.

The Truth of Sin

If sin were only disobedience, that is, the deviation from a norm, the damage could be repaired forthwith by obedience, and the problem of destiny would be solved by "composure." In reality, however, sin, in the strict sense, is "enmity against God," that is, active opposition to the will of God, which, to an equal degree, is active against sin. God replies to sin with a judgment that can terminate only in our death.

Werner Elert, *The Structure of Lutheranism* [CPH, 1962], p. 27

Man is by nature unable to want God to be God. Indeed, he himself wants to be God, and does not want God to be God.

Martin Luther, AE 31:10

Lutheran theology is nothing if it is not realistic! Like the Scriptures, Lutheran theology does not start with notions about human freedom and the potential (great or small) that human beings have. Theologies that start with assumptions about human freedom end up in bondage. Lutheran theology begins with man's bondage in sin and ends up with the glorious liberty of the Gospel. The bondage to sin is not a slight defect that can be corrected by appropriate self-discipline. Neither is it a sickness that can be cured by the appropriation of the medication of regular doses of God's grace. Sin is alienation from the Creator and carries with it God's verdict of guilt and a divinely-imposed death sentence. To be a sinner is to be held captive in death and condemnation. The distance between God and humanity is not the gap between the infinite and the finite, but between a holy God who is the judge and man who is the guilty defendant.

1. How is the captivating power of sin described in Ephesians 2:1–10?

Self-Deception Is the Enemy of the Truth

2. Denial is the polar opposite of confession. According to 1 John 1:8 and 10, what does the denial of sin demonstrate?

3. How does the prophet describe the depth of our self-deception in Jeremiah 17:9–10?

4. How does Psalm 32:3–5 depict the results of the failure to confess sin?

5. Read the confession of sins in the Divine Service. How does the confessional prayer identify our sin?

6. Some argue that Confession and Absolution should be omitted from the worship service because this practice immediately "tells people how bad they are" and that the service should instead begin with something more upbeat and affirming. How is this displacement of Confession and Absolution a confusion of Law and Gospel?

7. Note how 1 John 1:8–9 is used in the Divine Service. How does this promise of God give us the courage to confess our sin?

The Clarity of Confession

In the confession of sins, whether in the liturgy, before our pastor, to a Christian brother or sister, or in our prayers, we do not make excuses for our sins or whimper and whine over their bitter consequences in our lives. Instead, we confess them—we acknowledge that God's judgment on our sin is altogether true and right. He, is indeed, justified in His judgment (see Psalm 51:4–5). We name sin for what it is, recognizing that it merits God's temporal and eternal punishment. When we confess our sins, we are not telling God something that He does not already know. Before Him there are no secrets. He sees into the deepest recesses of the human soul. Confession is not for God's sake but for our own sake, that we might know our sin for what it is.

8. One of the helpful features of individual confession (see *LSB*, pp. 292–293) before our pastor is that we actually name our sins. While it is not possible or necessary to enumerate each and every sinful thought, word, or deed, how does the naming of specific sins give clarity to confession?

9. How does the Lord's Prayer keep us from self-deception when it comes to sin?

God's Righteousness Is Our Forgiveness

The apostle John does not stop with the confession of sin but moves quickly to the promise of the Gospel that God will forgive the sins of those who confess. This forgiveness is no sentimental attitude of God toward sinners but the work of God, who in His faithfulness and justice actually speaks words that deliver what they promise: pardon and cleansing for Jesus' sake.

10. Read 1 John 1:7. What cleanses us from all sin?

11. How does the Absolution demonstrate God's righteousness? See Romans 3:21–26 and Galatians 3:10–14.

Spiritual Exercises

- North American culture seems to have lost the ability to speak about sin. Sin's target is God, and we wish to think of ourselves as autonomous, accountable only to self. As you read or listen to the news this week, note how other categories are substituted for sin. Why are these categories inadequate? What are the implications for Christian witness as we speak God's Law and Gospel to unbelievers?
- Meditate on the hymn, "Alas, My God, My Sins Are Great" (*LW* 232) along with Psalm 90. Pray Psalm 90 each day this week. If you have time, you may also wish to read Luther's commentary on this psalm (see AE 13:75–141). Luther says of this psalm: "In a magnificent manner, therefore, he [Moses] performs the ministry of the Law; he depicts death in the most repulsive colors and in this way demonstrates that God's wrath is the cause of our death. Yes, he shows that even before we die physically, we have been put to death and are overwhelmed with dreadful miseries" (AE 13:77).
- Keep a journal of biblical passages that extol and magnify the greatness of the gift of the Gospel in light of the depth of our sin.

Point to Remember

If You, O LORD, should mark iniquities, O Lord, who could stand? But with You there is forgiveness, that You may be feared. Psalm 130:3–4

To prepare for "The Truth of the Law," read 2 Samuel 11:1–12:15.

The Truth of the Law

When Law and Gospel are improperly distinguished, both are undermined. Separated from the Law, the Gospel gets absorbed into an ideology of tolerance in which indiscriminateness is equated with grace. Separated from the Gospel, the Law becomes an insatiable demand hammering away at the conscience until it destroys a person. When Law and Gospel are properly distinguished, however, both are established. The Law can be set forth in its full-scale demand, so that it lights the way to order and through the work of the Spirit drives us to Christ. The Gospel can be declared in all of its purity, so that forgiveness of sins and deliverance from the powers of death and the devil are bestowed in the presence of our crucified and risen Lord.

James A. Nestingen, "Distinguishing Law and Gospel: A Functional View" *Concordia Journal* 22:1 (January 1996), p. 27

As soon as reason and the Law are joined, faith immediately loses its virginity.

Martin Luther, AE 26:113

Postmodernism is about "truth decay," or so we are told. But the truth of God's Law will not go away even if it is not recognized or denied. The Law just keeps on irrevocably doing its work, putting sinners to death: "Therefore, just as sin came into the world through one man, and death through sin, and so death spread to all men because all sinned" (Romans 5:12). As we have seen, you may call the God of truth a liar by insisting that you are without sin, but such an accusation only confirms the Law's verdict. Law and Gospel are at work in Confession and Absolution as the Law brings us to acknowledge our sin and the Gospel gifts the broken sinner with the forgiveness of sins. The unflinching and irrevocable truth of the Law is that all have sinned and are under God's condemnation. Only where this truth is made plain will sinners be able to hear God's ultimate truth:

the good news that, in Jesus Christ, God is not out to drive sinners into hell, but to make them alive through His death on the cross.

12. Read 2 Samuel 11:1–13. How did David sin in thought, word, and deed in this episode?

Cover-up or Confession?

13. How does David attempt to deal with his sin of adultery? How do you see David's attempt repeated in contemporary life?

14. What does David do when his scheme to locate the fatherhood of Bathsheba's child with Uriah fails?

15. Unconfessed sin is not static. It has an entangling dynamic all of its own. How does David's failure to confess his adultery lead to even greater sin?

16. How does this unveil David's unbelief?

17. How is David dismissive of the reality of sin in 2 Samuel 11:22–25? How is this a temptation for us as well?

18. What is God's evaluation of David in 2 Samuel 11:27?

The Law Makes a Direct Hit

Adam and Eve learned that you may run from the Creator but you cannot hide. Before God (*coram deo)* no secrets are hid. With its laser-like precision, the Law does not miss its intended target: the sinner secure in his or her sin. With inerrant accuracy, the Law on Nathan's lips, like the knife in the hand of a skilled surgeon, cuts deep into David's flesh so that the cancer of his heart can no longer be ignored. The parable of the wealthy rancher who steals his poor neighbor's pet lamb is a picture of David's own wretchedness. When David says that "the man who has done this deserves to die" (2 Samuel 12:5), he is speaking the terrible truth about himself.

19. What can we learn from Nathan about *how* we are to speak God's Law to secure sinners?

20. What does Nathan's preaching of the Law do to David?

A Word That Answers the Law

The Law renders David helpless. He cannot undo his adultery or bring back murdered Uriah from the grave. David can only confess, that is, agree with God's verdict that he is the man that God's Law declares him to be—the lustful adulterer and the plotting murderer whose hands are stained with Uriah's blood. Once the Law has done its work, Nathan does not hesitate to speak the Absolution, words from God that do what they say—they remove David's sin from him. They are words that now judge him forgiven and promise him life instead of the death that his sin deserves.

21. What is David's confession in 2 Samuel 12:13? Who has he sinned against?

22. What does the Absolution do for David?

Spiritual Exercises

- Use Luther's explanation of the Ten Commandments in the Small Catechism as a tool for self-examination under God's Law.
- Meditate on Luther's catechetical hymn on the Ten Commandments, "These Are the Holy Ten Commands" (*LSB 581; ELH* 490; *CW* 285; *LW* 331; *TLH* 287). How might this hymn, used in tandem with the explanation of the commandments in the catechism, help you in preparing for confession?
- Give thanks for the Gospel by praying, "Salvation Unto Us Has Come" (*LSB* 555; *ELH* 227; *CW* 390; *LW* 355; *LBW* 297; *TLH* 377).

Point to Remember

Now we know that whatever the law says it speaks to those who are under the law, so that every mouth may be stopped, and the whole world may be held accountable to God. For by works of the law no human being will be justified in His sight, since through the law comes knowledge of sin. Romans 3:19–20

To prepare for "The Truth of Repentance," read Psalm 51.

℘

The Truth of Repentance

But repentance consists of acknowledging everything that is mine is sin. You will never acknowledge this by using reason. But Christ commands that repentance be preached in his name: "So that you are justified in your sentence and blameless when you pass judgment." This is repentance, and at the same time you have the forgiveness of sins, because you acknowledge your sins and you are a true Jew and confess according to the Word of God that everything is sin. This is not according to reason, which says: "If I perform external righteousness, then it is not sin."

The 1529 Holy Week Sermons of Dr. Martin Luther
[CPH, 1999], pp. 165–66

"When our Lord and Master Jesus Christ said, 'Repent' [Matt. 4:17], he willed the entire life of the believer to be one of repentance" (AE 31:25). So wrote Luther in the very first of his Ninety-five Theses. Repentance is not an occasional guest in the Christian life, an episode of sorrow after a season of sin. The Christian is constantly living in repentance and faith, dying daily to sin and being made alive to walk by faith in the newness of life that is found only in Christ Jesus. Repentance is more than feeling sorrow for your sins, although as Paul puts it, "godly grief produces a repentance" (2 Corinthians 7:10). To repent is to be rendered defenseless before God, stripped of every self-justifying excuse that the old Adam can muster. To repent is to die to your sin. It is to see your sin as God sees it.

23. In verse 2 of Psalm 51, David prays that God would cleanse him from his sin. What is the significance of the other two synonyms for sin in verses 1 and 2?

God Does the Turning

24. How does David's prayer recognize that his salvation is completely the work of the triune God?

25. What does verse 5 teach us about sin?

26. Recalling our study of 1 John 1:8–10, what is the nature of the "truth in the inward being" and the "wisdom in the secret heart" (v. 6)?

27. In verse 8, David describes his bones as being broken. Who has broken his bones? What does this mean?

28. What kind of cleansing is David asking for in verse 7?

29. The catechism states that "confession has two parts." What are the two parts of confession? How are these two parts reflected in Psalm 51?

The Joy of Repentance

Repentance is a turning *from* sin and a turning *to* the mercy of God in Jesus Christ. Crushed by the Law, we are restored by the Gospel. The Apology of the Augsburg Confession reminds us that the Law can kill but it cannot vivify: "So in the preaching of repentance, it is not enough to preach the Law, or the Word that convicts of sin. The Law works wrath and only accuses. The Law terrifies consciences, because consciences never are at rest unless they hear God's voice clearly promising the forgiveness of sins. So the Gospel must be added, that for Christ's sake sins are forgiven and that we obtain the forgiveness of sins by faith in Christ" (Ap V 136). There is joy in repentance because of the Gospel alone.

30. Where do we hear the joy and gladness that David speaks of in verse 8?

31. How does God restore us to the joy of salvation? Also see Luke 15:7, 10.

Unlocked Lips

Jesus says that it is not what goes into a man that makes him unclean but rather that which comes out of him (see Matthew 15:11). We know what came out of David's mouth when he opened his own lips: the schemes to protect himself by arranging for Uriah's death, and the evasive and self-defensive speech that Uriah's death is just another casualty of war (see 2 Samuel 11:25). The only language that comes naturally to the sinner is that of the lie. Only when the Law silences the tongue made unclean by sin can lips be unloosed to speak the truth about self and about God. When God opens lips, then the truth is spoken—both the painful truth of our sin and the merciful truth that God seeks the life, not the death, of the sinner.

32. What happens when the Lord opens our lips? Contrast this with what happens when we open our mouths to speak.

33. What is the broken heart that God will not despise?

Spiritual Exercises

- Over the next seven days, pray each of the penitential psalms: 51; 6; 32; 38; 102; 130; and 143. As you pray these psalms, keep a journal to record your reflections on each individual psalm. In your journal, answer these three questions: (1) How is the Law at work in the psalm? (2) How does the psalm proclaim the Gospel? (3) Which petition of the Lord's Prayer is best reflected in each psalm?
- Commit to memory the words of Psalm 30:4–5 and use them as your personal prayer in thanksgiving for holy Absolution.
- Pray "To Thee, Omniscient Lord of All" (*LSB* 613; *LW* 234; *LBW* 310; *TLH* 318), noting the similarities of this hymn with Psalm 51.

Point to Remember

Repent, for the kingdom of heaven is at hand. Matthew 3:2

To prepare for "The Truth of Jesus, the Friend of Sinners," read Mark 2:1–17.

The Truth of Jesus, the Friend of Sinners

The earthly righteousness ceases and does not stand the test. But there must be One who is eternally over death and devil. For this reason Paul will not tolerate that Christians be perplexed in the conscience. It is the greatest skill: a Christian must be protected so that no one nails a law to her or his conscience and heart. You must have this skill if you want to believe in Christ. This is over all laws. If a hundred thousand sins fell on you today, you would still have to say, I know of none because Christ, who is subject to neither sin nor death, is risen from the dead.

The 1529 Holy Week Sermons of Dr. Martin Luther [CPH, 1999], p. 141

A crippled man is brought to Jesus. Behind the physical paralysis, there is a deeper bondage than confinement to the bed. Where is God in all of this? Luther often commented that a person has God as he or she imagines Him to be. What can this paralyzed man imagine about God? What can he conclude about God? Is God angry with him? Is this disease the heavy hand of God punishing him for some transgression? Is God oblivious to his plight, so far removed from him, in majesty and might, as to be unconcerned with his misery? We are not told anything about the inner thoughts of this nameless man. We do see Jesus speaking words of Absolution that forgive his sin and set him on his feet. Absolution disrupts the old order of sin and death. It is a word of powerful pardon that sets the captive free and causes the lame to walk. (See Isaiah 35:4–6.)

34. What is surprising about Jesus' words to the paralytic in Mark 2:5?

Who Is Jesus?

35. What do the words of verse 5 tell us about Jesus?

36. Why do the scribes conclude that Jesus' words are blasphemy rather than blessing?

37. How does Mark 2:13–17 serve as a commentary on Jesus' action in the Absolution of the paralytic?

38. Adolph Koeberle has described Jesus' approach to "tax collectors and sinners" as the embodiment of the forensic justification described by Paul in Romans 4:1–5 (see *The Quest for Holiness*, p. 57). How is this so?

39. This text points ahead to Calvary. Read Luke 23:39–43. How does Jesus show Himself the friend of sinners to the dying thief?

40. What are the implications of this text for the mission of the Church?

The Authority of the Absolution

Jesus speaks unexpected words. He says to the paralytic: "My son, your sins are forgiven." With these words, Jesus shows Himself to be the Savior. His greeting is the vehicle for mercy. The kingdom of Christ is in the sentence "your sins are forgiven"; in these words there is no demand, no Law, and no works. Jesus' words give the paralyzed man nothing that he must do to attain health. The Lord comes not to provide him with a regimen for physical therapy or a plan of spiritual renewal that he is to work at to help him cope with his misfortune. Calling him "son," Jesus shows Himself to be there for this man as His Helper and Savior. He has not come to mock him in his infirmity or crush him with condemnation, but rather He has come as his Lord with words of peace and Absolution: "My son, your sins are forgiven you."

41. According to Mark 2:10, Jesus speaks the Absolution to show His authority. What is this authority? See Daniel 7:13–14; Mark 14:61–64; and Matthew 28:18.

42. Sometimes visitors to a Lutheran church service are offended by the pastor saying: "As a called and ordained servant of Christ, and by His authority, I therefore forgive you all your sins in the name of the Father and of the Son and of the Holy Spirit." How might Mark 2:10 be helpful in answering their objection?

A Physician for the Sick

Forgiveness of sins is offensive on several levels. It is an offense against the rules of justice that insist each one should get what he deserves. It is also offensive in that it is only declared to sinners. Forgiveness of sins assumes that the recipient of the Absolution is indeed a sinner. The self-righteous have no need for the righteousness of Christ, the righteousness of faith bestowed in the Absolution. But for those who know their sin, the forgiveness of sins is good news.

43. How is Absolution different from attitudes of tolerance or acceptance that are often used as substitutes for forgiveness in our culture?

44. The Swedish theologian Gustaf Wingren once preached a sermon on this text in which he noted that there are really two miracles here. One is the divine healing granted through the forgiveness of sins. The other, Wingren said, is that the man picked up his bed and went home. He did not retreat to a monastery or go off on a religious tour to give his testimony! What does this tell us about the power of the forgiveness of sins?

Spiritual Exercises

- Review Luther's Explanation to the Second Article of the Creed in the Catechism. If you have not already done so, learn it by heart.
- Review the Divine Service, marking every place where worshipers confess the person and work of Christ for sinners (e.g., the *Agnus Dei* confesses Christ as the Lamb of God, etc.).
- Learn Galatians 2:20 by heart.
- Meditate on this comment from Luther's 1531 commentary on Galatians as you think about how the Lord would use you to comfort penitent sinners: "I wish that you students of Sacred Scripture would equip yourselves with such parables, in order to retain the distinction between Law and Gospel better, namely, that trying to be justified by the Law is like counting money out of an empty purse, eating and drinking from an empty dish and cup, looking for strength and riches where there is nothing but weakness and poverty, laying a burden upon someone who is already oppressed to the point of collapse, trying to spend a hundred gold pieces and not having even a pittance, taking clothing away from a naked man, imposing even greater weakness and

poverty upon someone who is sick and needy, etc." (AE 26:406–7).

Point to Remember

Now the tax collectors and sinners were all drawing near to hear Him. And the Pharisees and the scribes grumbled, saying, "This man receives sinners and eats with them." Luke 15:1–2

To prepare for "The Truth of the Absolution," read John 20:19–23.

ɞ

The Truth of the Absolution

The other part of Confession is the Absolution, which the priest speaks in God's place, and which therefore is nothing other than God's Word with which He comforts and strengthens our hearts against the sinful conscience.

Martin Luther, "An Open Letter to Those in Frankfurt on the Main"
Concordia Journal 16:4 (October 1990), p. 345

Dear God, what consolation can a weak conscience receive from a pastor, when it does not believe that these very words are the consolation of God himself, his Word, his doctrine. Therefore, we conclude that God works through his Word or not at all.

Luther, quoted by Reinhard Slenczka "Luther and Paul"
Concordia Journal 32:3 (July 2006), p. 311

Jesus is risen from the dead. But the disciples are still in confusion. They are hidden away in the upper room. It is more than a lock that keeps them in seclusion on Easter evening, for they are held in bondage by fear and uncertainty. Then Jesus appears speaking words of peace and showing them the marks of the nails and spear still present in His resurrected body. But this is more than just an appearance. Jesus speaks His benediction of peace a second time and with this word of peace institutes the Office of the Holy Ministry. He makes His disciples His apostles (sent ones), sending them even as He was sent from the Father. Their work is now to speak Jesus' words, forgiving the sins of the penitent and retaining the sins of the impenitent. Here the Office of the Keys is set in motion, so that you might have the fruits of Jesus' death, the peace that was made in His sacrificial death. That peace is nothing less than the forgiveness of your sins.

45. What is the relationship between the death and resurrection of Jesus and the forgiveness of sins? See Romans 4:22–25; 2 Corinthians 5:18–21; and Colossians 1:19–20.

In the Stead and by the Command of Christ

46. Review the Office of the Keys in the catechism. By whose authority do pastors forgive sins?

47. The Agenda suggests that when pastors hear Confession and speak the Absolution, they wear their vestments. What does this liturgical practice teach us?

48. What sins are we to confess before the pastor according to the catechism?

49. Look at Article XXV of the Augsburg Confession in the appendix (p. 67) of this study. What argument does the Augsburg Confession make for the retention of private confession?

50. Review the excerpts from Luther's "Exhortation to Confession" included in his Large Catechism (see appendix). What abuses does Luther identify in Roman Catholic teaching regarding private confession? How does Luther envision the restoration of private con-

fession in the Reformation churches? Why do you think private confession has fallen into disuse in many of our Lutheran churches?

51. What is the point of Luther's question in the Catechism's confessional rite, "Do you believe that my forgiveness is God's forgiveness?"

Forgiven!

One of the great blessings of private or individual confession is that the penitent hears the Gospel in a way that is unmistakably personal. When the pastor acting in the stead and by the command of the Lord says, "I forgive you all your sins," he is not just talking about forgiveness nor is he proclaiming forgiveness in a general sort of way that may or may not be applicable to you. Herein lies the powerful consolation that Jesus is Lord for you. It is your sins that are forgiven, for the One who is the Truth incarnate does not lie or deceive.

52. In the Lutheran ordination rite, the pastor pledges that he will never divulge the sin that is confessed to him. Even the state may not invade into the sacred trust, for in confession the sins are rendered to God, not man. See Matthew 22:17–22. What does God do with the sins rendered unto Him in confession? See Psalm 103:12.

53. When we confess our sins, they lie buried in Christ's empty tomb. Christians are not to live as grave robbers who exhume the rot of sin that God has crucified and buried with Christ. How does the Absolution serve to comfort you when the devil creates what Luther

call *anfechtung*, bringing to your memory sins that God has judged forgiven? See 1 John 3:19–24 and Isaiah 6:1–7.

Retained!

There is only one way to receive Absolution and that is by repentance and faith. Those who harden themselves against God's Law and insist that they have no need for the forgiveness of sins are left with their sins. Pastors have the responsibility of retaining the sins of the unrepentant, that is, of announcing to them that they are stuck with their sins and the terrible judgment that unbelief brings. This word of unrelenting Law must be preached to sinners who are secure and comfortable in living with their sins, apart from the mercy and grace of God in Christ Jesus, so that they might recognize their sin for what it is, repent, and hear the word of forgiveness.

54. Foundational to the Office of the Keys are the words of Jesus in Matthew 16:18–19. What does this text tell us about the binding and loosing of sins?

55. Read Matthew 18:15–20 and Galatians 6:1. What do these passages tell us about the evangelical goal of Church discipline?

Spiritual Exercises

- Review the order for individual Confession and Absolution in *Lutheran Service Book* or another Lutheran hymnal. Consider making use of this gift with your pastor.
- Learn the words of the Absolution in the Divine Service by heart so that, when the devil tempts you to doubt that these words were spoken to you by your pastor as Christ's servant, you may

recall them and use them to quench his devilish accusation.

- Study the Divine Service and identify the places where an Absolution is spoken, in addition to the formula of Absolution in the confession of sins.
- Meditate on these words from Luther's lectures on Hebrews: "For since it [conscience] cannot change a sin committed in the past and in any way avoid the future wrath, it cannot escape being distressed and troubled, no matter where it turns. Nor is it freed from these difficulties except through the blood of Christ; and if it looks at Him through faith, it believes and realizes that its sins have been washed away and taken away in Him. Thus through faith it is at the same time purified and made calm, so that out of joy over the remission of sins it no longer dreads punishments" (AE 29:209).

Point to Remember

As far as the east is from the west, so far does He remove our transgressions from us. Psalm 103:12

To prepare for "The Truth of Freedom in the Forgiveness of Sins," read Colossians 3:1–17.

The Truth of Freedom in the Forgiveness of Sins

Our faith in Christ does not free us from works but from false opinions concerning works, that is, from the foolish presumption that justification is acquired by works. Faith redeems, corrects, and preserves our consciences so that we know that righteousness does not consist in works, although works neither can nor ought to be wanting; just as we cannot be without food and drink and all the works of this mortal body, yet our righteousness is not in them, but in faith; and yet those works of the body are not to be despised or neglected on that account.

Martin Luther, AE 31:372–373

Christians are both forgiven and forgiving people. The gift of God's pardon received through faith in Christ Jesus is transmitted in love to those who sin against us. Where there is no forgiveness of sins, there is only bondage to sin. Christ Jesus has set us free from the prison house of sin and the domain of death by a word that liberates us from the tyranny of those powers that would destroy and damn us. In Christ Jesus, there is no condemnation (see Romans 8:1).

56. Read Colossians 3:1–17 carefully. Where does Paul say that our lives are hidden? Where did this concealment take place? See Colossians 2:11–15.

Freedom From and Freedom For

57. Read John 8:31–38. What is ironic about the claim of the Jews in verse 33 never to have been enslaved by anyone? How is Absolution the truth that sets us free?

58. Christian freedom is liberty, not license. By the blood of Christ, we are set free from the guilt of sin, the condemnation of the Law, and the sting of God's wrath. What does Paul say that baptismal death spells a freedom from in Colossians 3:5–11?

59. How does Paul describe the life of repentance in Colossians 3:9–10? Compare this text with Romans 6:1–11.

60. The freedom of the Absolution entails vocation or calling. We are called by the Gospel to live in Christ by faith and in the neighbor by love. How is this twofold calling reflected in Colossians 3:12–17?

61. Read Galatians 5:1. How is this section of Colossians a commentary on the freedom that we have in Christ?

62. In Colossians 3:15, Paul speaks of the rulership of God's peace in the life of the believer. Recall our study of the relationship of the peace of God to the forgiveness of sins in the last session. Martin

Luther once commented that the *Pax Domini* ("The peace of the Lord be with you always") in the Divine Service is "a public absolution of the sins of the communicants, the true voice of the gospel announcing remission of sins, and therefore the one and most worthy preparation for the Lord's Table, if faith holds to these words as coming from the mouth of Christ himself" (AE 53:28–29). Where else is the peace of God specifically proclaimed in the liturgy?

Living in the Absolution

The catechism's explanation to the Fifth Petition reminds us that we daily implore our Father for the forgiveness of our sins because "we daily sin much and surely deserve nothing but punishment." The Christian life is a constant struggle with the devil, the world, and our own proud flesh. It is a dangerous illusion to believe that we can live without the forgiveness of sins. The forgiveness of sins is never past tense; it is always a present-tense reality as we constantly crawl back to our Baptism in repentance and faith. It is a spiritual danger signal of the first order if a Christian begins to think of himself or herself as something other than a forgiven sinner. For we are always on this side of the resurrection of the dead, *simul iustus et peccator,* at one and the same time both righteous and sinful.

63. Read Romans 7:7–25. How does Paul demonstrate our constant need for Absolution?

64. As we have already observed, the liturgy is packed with the forgiveness of sins. God delights in extending His pardon to us in more than one way. Paul tells us that we are to let the word of Christ dwell in us richly as we teach and admonish one another "singing psalms and hymns and spiritual songs" (Colossians 3:16). At the beginning of this session, we prayed Luther's great hymn, "Dear Christians, One and All Rejoice" (*LSB* 556; *ELH* 378; *CW* 377; *LW* 353;

LBW 299; *TLH* 387). How does this hymn let Christ's word dwell in us, literally singing the forgiveness of sins into our ears and hearts?

Vocation

When God calls us to faith by the Gospel, He does not call us out of the world but to a life of love that is lived within His creation. Yet it is precisely in our worldly callings that we sin. Our sin drives us back to the Divine Service and to Absolution. When we examine ourselves in preparation for Confession, Luther wisely counsels us in the catechism: "Consider your place in life according to the Ten Commandments: Are you a father, mother, son, daughter, . . ." Where our place in life (vocation) intersects with God's Law, there we see our sin. Vocation keeps us from ever outgrowing the Lord's Prayer—and Luther's evening prayer, for that matter, where we ask God "to forgive me all my sins where I have done wrong and graciously keep me this night."

65. It is within our vocations that we sin against our neighbor and are sinned against. God daily and richly forgives us our sin. He has also put the words of forgiveness on our lips. What does Paul direct all Christians to do in Colossians 3:13?

66. According to Colossians 3:17, what is the outcome of the words of Christ's forgiveness?

Spiritual Exercises

- *The Hammer of God* by Bo Giertz is a great novel that illustrates the freedom of the forgiveness of sins that we have in Christ. Read this novel for your own edification.

- Pray the Fifth Petition along with the catechism explanation, naming a person whom you are struggling to forgive.
- Use Compline—Prayer at the Close of the Day (*LSB* 253–59; *LW*, pp. 263–69) as your evening devotion with your family, noting the way that this service has us confessing our sins and speaking God's forgiveness to each other.
- When we confess our sins, we are returning to our Baptism. Pray the following baptismal hymns each day this week, noting how the hymn teaches us to rejoice in the present-tense reality of Baptism:

  S. "The Gifts Christ Freely Gives" (*LSB* 602)
  M. "All Christians Who Have Been Baptized" (*LSB* 596)
  T. "Baptized into Your Name Most Holy" (*LSB* 590; *ELH* 242; *CW* 294; *LW* 224; *LBW* 192; *TLH* 298)
  W. "God's Own Child, I Gladly Say It" (*LSB* 594; *ELH* 246)
  T. "Once in the Blest Baptismal Waters" (*LSB* 598; *TLH* 598)
  F. "O Gracious Lord, with Love Draw Near" (*LSB* 599)
  S. "Baptismal Waters Cover Me" (*LSB* 616)

Point to Remember

For freedom Christ has set us free; stand firm therefore, and do not submit again to a yoke of slavery. Galatians 5:1

Leader Guide

Leaders, please note the different abilities of your Bible study participants. Some will easily find the many passages listed in this study. Others will struggle to find even the "easy" passages. To help everyone participate, team up members of the class. For example, if a question asks you to look up several passages, assign one passage to one group, the second to another, and so on. Divide up the work! Let participants present the different answers they discover.

Each topic is divided into four easy-to-use sections.

Focus introduces participants to key concepts that will be discovered in the session.

Inform guides participants into Scripture to uncover biblical truth.

Connect enables participants to apply that which is learned in Scripture to their lives.

Vision provides participants with practical suggestions for extending the theme of the lesson out of the classroom and into the world.

The Truth of Sin

Objectives

By the power of the Holy Spirit working through God's Word, participants will (1) see more clearly the biblical teaching of the depth of human sin as the evil and inborn failure to fear, love, and trust in God above all things, which we have inherited from Adam and daily express in thought, word, and deed; (2) recognize and address contemporary denials of sin that would undermine the atonement of Christ; (3) learn how to name sin for what it is; (4) see God's answer to sin in the forgiveness obtained by Christ's sacrificial death and bestowed in the Gospel.

Opening Worship

Father of mercies and God of all consolation, come to the aid of your people, turning us from our sin to live for You alone. Give us the power of Your Holy Spirit that we may attend to Your Word, confess our sins, receive Your forgiveness, and grow into the fullness of Your Son Jesus Christ, our Lord (*LW*, p. 308).

Sing "From Depths of Woe I Cry to Thee" (*LSB* 607; *ELH* 452; *CW* 305; *LW* 230; *LBW* 295; *TLH* 329).

Focus

1. Paul describes life apart from faith in Christ Jesus as being dead in trespasses and sins. Just as a corpse cannot will itself to be alive, so those who are spiritually dead must be made alive by a power that is outside of the self. Sin places us in a prison from which we cannot escape. We are made alive and liberated by the promise of the Gospel, which creates faith. The leader here may wish to refer to Article II of the Augsburg Confession.

Self-Deception Is the Enemy of the Truth

2. To deny that we are sinners demonstrates that we are sinners, for the essence of sin is unbelief. Unbelief calls God a liar.

3. The human heart is deceitful above all things. That is, the human heart cannot be trusted, for it is the center of that inborn mistrust of God called sin. As the heart is a veritable cesspool of anger, adultery, pride, and murder (see Mark 7:21–23), its directives are not to be trusted. God has given us something far more sure and certain than the fickle heart. He has given us His Word.

4. The psalmist speaks of sin as a disease that causes anguish in body and soul as he poetically describes a wasting away of the bones. The heavy hand of God's wrath is unrelenting over and against the one who attempts to deny his sin. "Sin has its own hidden law of gravitation" says Adolph Koeberle (*The Quest for Holiness* [Augsburg, 1938], p. 216), as it pulls the sinner ever deeper into either denial or despair. When sin is not acknowledged, the sinner is hardened in his or her denial or is plunged into despair that will not trust in Christ's forgiveness.

5. The confessional prayers in the liturgies of both *Lutheran Service Book* and *Lutheran Worship* confess that we are guilty of original sin as "we are by nature sinful and unclean" and that we have sinned against God in "thought, word, and deed." We have sinned by commission and omission, that is, "by what we have done and by what we have left undone." The prayer is anchored in the Ten Commandments, especially the First Commandment. We have not loved God with "our whole heart and we have not loved our neighbors as ourselves." Here the leader may also wish to point out that when we confess that we are poor, miserable sinners we are not making a statement about how we *feel* but rather that we are in need of divine mercy. On this point, see the excellent essay by C. S. Lewis, "Miserable Offenders" in *God in the Dock: Essays on Theology and Ethics*, where Lewis points out that the English word *miserable* is derived from the Latin word for one in need of mercy. Participants may also be directed to the confessional prayer in the order for individual Confession and Absolution in *Lutheran Service Book* and *Lutheran Worship* ("I have lived as if God did not matter . . .").

6. The liturgy starts with the reality that we are sinners. The Divine Service is a service that God renders to sinners, namely, proclaiming to them a Word of promise that raises the dead and feeding them with the meal of His New Testament, Christ's body and blood. Without the Law, there is no need for the Gospel. When the Service is turned into something other than God's vehicle for the delivery of His forgiveness, then we are left with our celebration, affirmation,

motivation, and so forth. All of that is finally in the category of the Law. Feeling affirmed is a poor substitute for being forgiven by Christ!

7. This text is used responsively in the Divine Service to prepare us for the confession of our sins. Without the confidence that God is the Lord who is merciful and promises to forgive the sins of all who repent, we would never come to confess our sins. The promise of God's merciful pardon for sinners gives us the courage to confess our sins.

The Clarity of Confession

8. Naming our sins individually is a guard against attempting to hold any sin outside of Christ's forgiveness. While it is true that it is impossible to enumerate every instance of sin (see Psalm 19:12), naming the sin acknowledges the truth of the Law's diagnosis. Naming our sins is not for God's benefit, but for our own. God sees us as we are. The problem is that we are easily seduced into self-deception and we evade the truth about ourselves. Naming our sins guards us against what Herman Bezzel described as a "general repentance" that he said is "the death of repentance" (quoted in Adolph Koeberle, *The Quest for Holiness* [Augsburg, 1938], 214). A "general repentance" acknowledges sin as a generic reality but fails to come to terms with the concrete reality of one's own sin. Luther's advice that each person should examine his or her life in light of their place in life (station in life, i.e., mother, child, worker, etc.) and the Ten Commandments is brought into the order of Individual Confession and Absolution in *Lutheran Service Book.* This helps us to rightly see our sin as God's Law intersects with the places where God has called us to live in faith and love.

9. Here the leader may want to walk through the catechism's explanations of each petition of the Lord's Prayer, noting how repentance and faith, Confession and Absolution, are implicit if not explicit in each. For example, we pray "hallowed be Thy name" as those who have profaned God's name. In praying "Thy kingdom come," we are praying that we might believe the Absolution. When we pray "Thy will be done on earth as it is in heaven," we are imploring God to deal with not only the evil plans and purposes of the world and the devil, but our own sinful nature. The Fourth Petition is a prayer against the unbelief that will not receive God's provisions with

thanksgiving. The Fifth Petition can only be prayed by sinners, for it is a prayer for the forgiveness of sins. In the Sixth Petition, we pray against the temptations that constantly assault us from the devil, the world, and our sinful nature. In the Seventh Petition, we are crying out for the final deliverance from sin. The "Amen" is uttered as the great word of faith—trust that God will indeed keep His promises.

God's Righteousness Is Our Forgiveness

10. The blood of Christ. Here the leader may wish to direct participants to review the catechism explanation to the Second Article, as it speaks of how Christ has redeemed us not with gold and silver but with His precious blood. This atonement is the basis for Absolution. Without Jesus' vicarious death for sinners, there would be no Absolution of sinners.

11. Absolution is the application of Christ's atonement to the sinner. It is spoken not on account of any righteousness on our part but by virtue of Christ's redeeming righteousness. It is a word that forgives sins because Christ was made sin for us on the cross, dying in our place so that we might be clothed with His righteousness. Without that atonement, there would be no Absolution. Christ was cursed for us so that in Him we might hear not God's curse, but His blessing. That blessing is Absolution. Absolution is justification by faith alone in action as God Himself is at work to raise to life those who have been killed by His Law. This comment of Luther is also helpful in clarifying the relationship between atonement and Absolution: "We treat of the forgiveness of sins in two ways. First, how it is achieved and won. Second, how it is distributed and given to us. Christ has achieved it on the cross, it is true. But he has not distributed or given it on the cross. He has not won it in the supper or sacrament. There he has distributed and given it through the Word, as also in the gospel, where it is preached. He has won it once for all on the cross. But the distribution takes place continuously, before and after, from the beginning to the end of the world" (AE 40:213–214).

The Truth of the Law

Objectives

By the power of the Holy Spirit working through God's Word, participants will (1) hone their skills in rightly distinguishing the Law from the Gospel; (2) see that the Law works to unveil sin, leaving the sinner dead and without excuse before God; (3) learn how to use the Law as the mirror that without error or delusion shows us the symptoms of our failure to fear, love, and trust in God above all things.

Opening Worship

O Lord, absolve Your people from their offenses that from the bonds of our sins, which by reason of our weakness we have brought upon us, we may be delivered by Your bountiful goodness; through Jesus Christ, Your Son, our Lord, who lives and reigns with You and the Holy Spirit, one God, now and forever (*LW*, p. 91).

Sing "The Law of God Is God and Wise" (*LSB* 579; *ELH* 492; *CW* 287; *LW* 329; *TLH* 295).

Focus

12. David's sin had its genesis in his sinful heart as he looked in lust on his neighbor's wife (11:2). He sends word to Bathsheba inviting her to the palace (11:3–4), and he has sexual intercourse with her (11:4–5). The adulterous desires of David's heart lead to words that scheme to secure another man's wife for himself and eventuate in the deed of adultery.

Cover-up or Confession?

13. David believes that he can handle this situation with a bit of ingenuity. He brings Uriah back from the front lines for "rest and recreation" in Jerusalem. This furlough from the battle will allow people to assume that, since Uriah was home, he must be the father of Bathsheba's child. Answers will vary as to contemporary parallels. Examples might include such things as a woman using murder (abortion) in

an attempt to conceal an adulterous affair. The leader should explain that when human beings do not trust in God's justification given by faith alone, they will inevitably seek to justify their own existence. For a helpful exposition of this point, see Oswald Bayer, *Living by Faith: Justification and Sanctification*, pages 1–26.

14. David hatches yet another plot to silence Uriah, who could potentially accuse him of sin. He devises a strategy that will lead to Uriah's death (see 11:14–21).

15. David gets himself ever deeper into sin as he will not suffer the humiliation of the old Adam entailed in repentance. Instead, he pursues a course of action that leads from adultery to murder. His sin becomes self-multiplying. One sin leads to yet another if the fatal chain reaction is not broken by repentance and forgiveness.

16. David is not fearing, loving, and trusting in God above all things. He fears the loss of reputation and position, perhaps, but he has no fear of God. He loves his own pleasure and security more than God. He trusts in his own ability to secure his future by well-laid schemes.

17. David treats his sin lightly. Soldiers die in war. Uriah was a soldier. Uriah died. David gives Joab the hollow comfort that Uriah's death is not worth worrying over. Answers will vary as to how this is a temptation also for us. Participants may think of examples of our cultural trivialization of sin or individual efforts to rationalize sin. It might also be pointed out that many in our day live under the illusion that they are autonomous—literally a law unto themselves. Right and wrong are viewed as a matter of personal choice.

18. God is displeased with David.

The Law Makes a Direct Hit

19. Nathan lets the word of preaching reveal David's sin. A head-on confrontation might have backfired for Nathan. Instead, Nathan tells a parable in such a way as to let the Law loose with full force. David is brought to see himself in Nathan's parable, as it is a mirror of David's own existence. The parable breaks through his security systems and catches him off guard. Here also note Luther: "Therefore the proper and absolute use of the Law is to terrify with lightning (as on Mt. Sinai), thunder, and the blare of the trumpet, with a thunderbolt to burn and crush that brute which is called the presumption of righteousness. Hence God says through Jeremiah

(23:29): 'My Word is a hammer which breaks the rock in pieces.' For as long as the presumption of righteousness remains in a man, there remain immense pride, self-trust, smugness, hate of God, contempt of grace and mercy, ignorance of the promises and of Christ. The proclamation of free grace and the forgiveness of sins does not enter his heart and understanding, because that huge rock and solid wall, namely, the presumption of righteousness by which the heart itself is surrounded, prevents this from happening. Therefore this presumption of righteousness is a huge and a horrible monster. To break and crush it, God needs a large and powerful hammer, that is, the Law, which is the hammer of death, the thunder of hell, and the lightning of divine wrath. To what purpose? To attack the presumption of righteousness, which is a rebellious, stubborn, and stiff-necked beast. . . . Then the Law is being employed in its proper use and for its proper purpose. Then the heart is crushed to the point of despair. This use and function of the Law is felt by terrified and desperate consciences" (AE 26:310).

20. It convicts him of his sin. He sees himself as the man that he has just asserted deserves to die. He pronounces God's sentence on himself: guilty! Here the leader may also need to explain that, in the Scriptures, "guilt" is not a matter of emotional reaction to one's misdeeds. Instead, it is the forensic declaration of God through the Law. A criminal who is declared guilty by a judge in a courtroom may or may not have feelings of remorse. That is irrelevant, for the word of the judge has pronounced him guilty and he now must endure the penalty.

A Word That Answers the Law

21. David confesses that he has sinned against the Lord. The leader may wish to direct participants to Psalm 51:4 for further sharpening of this point. All sin is ultimately against the First Commandment. As the Lord hides Himself behind the mask of our neighbor, all sin is finally aimed at Him.

22. The Absolution that Nathan speaks to David declares two things. First, it announces that the Lord has taken away David's sin. Sin in the Scriptures has a location. It will either rest squarely on your own shoulders or it will be carried by the Lamb of God who takes away the sin of the world. In Absolution, Christ lifts the load from our backs and carries it in His own body. Second, the Absolution

proclaims to David that he will not die under the condemnation of His sin. He has confessed his sin and now he will live to confess the mercies and favor of the God who saved him. The Absolution is both pardon and the promise of the resurrection. It may be pointed out that the Apostles' Creed ties the forgiveness of sins to the resurrection of the body and life everlasting.

The Truth of Repentance

Objectives

By the power of the Holy Spirit working through God's Word, participants will (1) understand that repentance embraces the whole Christian life; (2) see the connection between Baptism and repentance; (3) themselves repent and trust the Gospel.

Opening Worship

Almighty and everlasting God, because You hate nothing you have made and forgive the sins of all who are penitent, create in us new and contrite hearts that we, worthily repenting our sins and acknowledging our wretchedness, may obtain from You, the God of all mercy, perfect remission and forgiveness; through Jesus Christ, Your Son our Lord, who lives and reigns with You and the Holy Spirit, one God, now and forever (*LW*, p. 32).

Sing "On Jordan's Bank the Baptist's Cry" (*LSB* 344; *ELH* 106; *CW* 16; *LW* 14; *LBW* 36; *TLH* 63).

Focus

23. Transgressions are the trespasses, the stepping over of the boundaries that God has established. Iniquity is the bitter unrighteousness of a spoiled creation that now gives evidence of death and decay. Each of these synonyms brings out a dimension of sin, as in unbelief it will not honor the Creator's boundaries (transgressions). Although sin appears to the eye and heart as so beautiful and sweet, it is actually ugly and diseased.

God Does the Turning

24. David implores God to carry the action of the verbs. David might wallow in self-pity, but only God can have mercy on him and blot out his transgressions (Psalm 51:1). Only God can wash David in such a way as to cleanse him from the filth of sin (vv. 2, 7). Only God

can create in David a new heart (v. 10) and restore to him the joy of salvation (v. 12).

25. All sin has as its target the living God. God is therefore blameless in His judgment. Here the leader might want to elaborate on how the old Adam always attempts a role reversal with God. In the Scriptures, God is the judge and man is the defendant. The old Adam tries to act as though he is the judge and God is the defendant. In our arrogance, we seek to justify our sins and make God accountable to our judgments!

26. God delights in the Amen of faith embedded in the heart and confessed with the lips. Without the Amen of faith, the confession of sins is impossible. Wisdom in the Scriptures is to see life from God's perspective. The wisdom that the Spirit teaches us is the wisdom of Christ crucified for the sins of the world. This is the wisdom of God. See 1 Corinthians 1:18–25.

27. God has crushed David's bones with the Law. Pulverized bones render him crippled, unable to pursue his foolish attempts at evading his sin and the God from whom no secrets are hid.

28. David is asking to be thoroughly cleansed, purged of his sins. He implores God to rid him of his sins, to wash them away that their presence might not pollute his life.

29. The first part is that we confess our sins. The second part is that "we receive absolution, that is, forgiveness from the pastor as from God Himself, not doubting but firmly believing that by it our sins are forgiven before God in heaven." Psalm 51 reflects the narrative of David that we have already studied from 2 Samuel 11–12. Verses 1–12 of Psalm 51 recount David's confession of his sin while verses 13–19 are a meditation on the blessing of the Absolution spoken by Nathan.

The Joy of Repentance

30. We hear this joy and gladness in the preaching of the forgiveness of sins as God declares to us the Good News that He has taken away our sin and restored us to life with Him through the blood of Christ.

31. By bringing us to Himself in repentance and faith. Absolution gives us the joy of the resurrection, for it brings us out of the death of sin into life with Christ. "The forgiveness of sins carries with it the power of the resurrection" (Adolph Koeberle, *The Quest for Ho-*

liness [Augsburg, 1938], p. 90). Here the leader may also refer to Romans 6:1–11. Christ suffered death *for* our sins on the cross. In Baptism we die *to* our sins. The baptismal life is the life of repentance and faith, of death and resurrection. Repentance does not end with the gloom of sin but in the promise of the glory of the resurrection.

Unlocked Lips

32. We speak the truth about Him and ourselves. This is in contrast with the rationalizations, self-justifications, and accusations that we by nature direct both at our neighbor and God Himself when we open our own mouths. Remember Adam's reaction in Genesis 3:12 where he blames both his wife and God for his sin.

33. The heart that God will not despise is the contrite heart—the heart that has been broken by sin and crushed by the Law and now looks to Christ alone for forgiveness. The broken heart is the heart that is severed from the object of its craving and split off from the idols for which it lived.

The Truth of Jesus, the Friend of Sinners

Objectives

By the power of the Holy Spirit working through God's Word, participants will (1) grow in their understanding that Jesus has redeemed us by His precious blood; (2) see that in the life and ministry of Jesus, God is justifying the ungodly; (3) give thanks for the gift of salvation won for us by the Lamb of God.

Opening Worship

Merciful and everlasting God the Father, who did not spare Your only Son but delivered Him up for us all that He might bear our sins on the cross, grant that our hearts may be so fixed with steadfast faith in our Savior that we may not fear the power of any adversaries; through Jesus Christ, our Lord, who lives and reigns with You and the Holy Spirit, one God, now and forever (*LW,* p. 43).

Sing "Jesus Sinners Doth Receive" (*LSB* 609; *CW* 304; *LW* 229; *LBW* 291; *TLH* 324).

Focus

34. Jesus speaks as only God can speak. He forgives sins right here on earth. The Jews expected God's vindication on the Last Day. Now Jesus speaks God's forgiveness ahead of time. The forgiveness of sins is not hidden away in an unknown future. Jesus proclaims it here and now.

Who Is Jesus?

35. He is the Lord who forgives sin. Here Jesus reveals the fatherly heart of God (as Luther liked to put it). Jesus addresses a crippled man as His son, pronouncing a Word of pardon that will accomplish what He promises.

36. They believed that since God alone can forgive sins, Jesus was claiming equality with God in this enactment of divine pardon. Hence, Jesus, in their minds, was blaspheming.

37. Here the Lord shows Himself to be the friend of sinners. He receives notorious outcasts into His fellowship, demonstrating that He came to call not the "righteous" but sinners. In this episode, we have an example of what Luther referred to as the theology of the cross in opposition to a theology of glory. The theology of glory operates according to the *opinion legis*, the opinion of the law, as it teaches that God rewards the righteous but punishes the unrighteous. Jesus turns this upside down as He goes to the cross to save those who should be condemned.

38. Tax collectors and sinners (see Mark 2:15–17) are obviously ungodly. Paul writes in Romans 4:1–5 that God justifies the ungodly not by works but through faith alone (also see Romans 5:6–11). As Luther liked to put it, Christ dwells only with sinners!

39. This is a fine illustration of Confession and Absolution at work. A dying thief who has no time for the amendment of his evil life says to his unrepentant companion in crime, "we are receiving the due reward of our deeds" (Luke 23:41), and then turns to Jesus with a plea for mercy, a request to be remembered in His kingdom. Jesus' words open heaven to this dying thug. The thief will be with his Lord in heaven.

40. The mission of the Church is to preach the Law and the Gospel, repentance and faith to all people, not just those whom we would judge to be likely candidates for salvation. The mission of the Church is directed toward real, flesh and blood sinners. It is not a program of church growth or cultural accommodation, but of the proclamation of the Gospel of the crucified and risen Lord. It involves the speaking of the Law to uncover and dethrone sin, the unbelief that delivers death, but ultimately the mission of the Church is to proclaim to sinners that God has reconciled them to Himself in Christ and that He forgives them their sin.

The Authority of the Absolution

41. Jesus exercises the authority that the Father has given to the Son of Man. It is the authority to forgive sins because the Son of Man is the One who has carried those sins to the cross and answered for them as our Brother. The sainted Gerhard Forde liked to explain that

in the Absolution the verdict of the Last Day slips out ahead of time. In other words, when we hear the Absolution now in time, we are hearing what all believers in Christ will hear on that final day when He returns to judge the living and the dead.

42. This is part and parcel of the Gospel. God has committed to His servants the ministry of reconciliation (see 2 Corinthians 5:18–21). As Christ's ambassadors, His ministers do not speak their own words, but the words of the One who sent them. Of those that He sends, Jesus says: "The one who hears you hears Me" (Luke 10:16). Jesus commissioned His apostles not merely to talk about the forgiveness of sins, but actually to forgive sins here and now (see John 20:23).

A Physician for the Sick

43. Absolution recognizes sin for what it is. Absolution does not deny the reality that sin is so much more than an errant attitude, a misspoken word, or a hurtful deed. Sin is not merely something that is socially inappropriate. Sin is unbelief enacted in countless ways. Tolerance would put up with the failures of others. Acceptance would ignore the condition that is delivering death. Neither toleration nor acceptance will deliver the sinner from the ultimate outcome of his or her sin. Both leave the sinner in sin and under the illusion of health while in reality they are fatally sick. One does not need the cross for tolerance and acceptance. Absolution necessitates the cross, for without the shedding of blood there is no forgiveness of sins.

44. The forgiveness of sins is not only an amnesty but a powerful pardon that enables us to live in the newness of life in those places where the Lord has put us. Forgiveness of sins does not draw the healed paralytic away from his home and family but sends him back there to live in faith and love.

The Truth of the Absolution

Objectives

By the power of the Holy Spirit working through God's Word, participants will (1) come to understand the gift of Absolution as justification by faith alone in action; (2) grow in their appreciation for the practice of private Confession and Absolution; (3) learn to trust Jesus' absolving words in Scripture, liturgy, sermon, and Sacrament.

Opening Worship

Almighty and ever-living God, since You have given exceedingly great and precious promises to those who believe, grant us so perfectly and without all doubt to believe in Your Son Jesus Christ that our faith in Your sight may never be reproved; through our Savior, Jesus Christ, who lives and reigns with You and the Holy Spirit, one God, now and forever (*LW,* p. 92).

Sing "'As Surely as I Live,' God Said" (*LSB* 614; *CW* 308; *LW* 235; *TLH* 331).

Focus

45. Without the atoning work of Jesus on the cross and His resurrection from the dead, we would be left desolate in sin, destined for death, and without hope. By His dying in our place, our sins are atoned for, and by His rising from the grave, we are justified. Absolution would be empty without the atoning work of Christ. Absolution is the application of the blood of Christ personally to you. With Jesus' words of forgiveness, He sprinkles you with His blood. This is signified by the pastor making the sign of the cross over you when he speaks the words of Absolution.

Here the leader should emphasize that God's verdict of forgiveness is true because of Christ's death and resurrection. The words of Robert Preus are helpful and to the point: "There is nothing fictional or untrue about this verdict. My justification is as true and valid as Christ's cursed death on the cross. . . . His verdict is effective: it accomplishes what it says. When he pronounces me righteous in Christ, then it is so, all accusations, inner doubts and empirical evidence to the contrary notwithstanding. Nor is God's verdict a mere possibility—to which I add my faith. And it will not be undone, just as Christ's incarnation, suffering and death cannot be undone" (Robert Preus, *Doctrine Is Life: Essays on Justification and the Lutheran Confessions* [CPH, 2006], p. 25).

In the Stead and by the Command of Christ

46. Pastors forgive sins not by their own authority but by the command and in the stead of Christ. Here the leader may also point participants to the Apology of the Augsburg Confession VIII 28, which teaches us that ministers do not represent their own persons but Christ.

47. The vestments cover up the man. His personal identity is not important, but the fact that he speaks Jesus' words is. The vestments serve as a uniform to remind both pastor and people of what he is here to do.

48. We confess before God that we are guilty of all sins, but before the pastor we confess only those sins that we know or feel in our hearts. At this point, participants should be reminded that their pastors have been taught not to be detectives, investigators, or judges, but shepherds and physicians of the soul. The pastor will not pry out of curiosity but only ask questions to better diagnose the sin so that the Absolution may be spoken.

49. The Augsburg Confession argues for the retention of private confession for the sake of the Absolution and the consolation that it brings to wounded conscience. Absolution is prized as God's "voice from heaven" to be received through faith alone.

50. Roman Catholic abuses of confession include the fact that it was made mandatory so that people were using it under coercion and out of fear. People were tortured by the requirement that they enumerate all their sins (an impossible task!). They were not taught the consoling benefits of the Absolution but left to rely on their own works for satisfaction. Luther envisions private confession standing alongside other forms of confession in evangelical churches: the confession made in the Lord's Prayer and the confession made to the neighbor against whom we have sinned (see James 5:16). Luther points out that it would be an abuse of Christian freedom to dispense

with private confession. It should be retained and used in the Church evangelically so that sinners might know the comfort of the Gospel.

There are, no doubt, many reasons why private confession has been neglected in present-day Lutheran church life. Already at the time of the Reformation, Luther identified those who mistakenly neglected private confession in the name of Christian freedom. In the seventeenth century, there was the powerful movement of Pietism, with its stress on the subjectivity of personal religious experience instead of the objective character of God's Gospel. Pietism was detrimental to the practice of private confession. Great Lutheran churchmen such as C. F. W. Walther, Wilhelm Loehe, and Theodore Kliefoth battled against this movement, urging Lutherans not to abandon private confession. For a very helpful summary of the place of private Confession and Absolution in Lutheran history, the leader may consult *Lutheran Worship: History and Practice* (edited by Fred Precht, pp. 322–386). There are other reasons that private confession has declined in contemporary Lutheran churches. Pastors have not always spent sufficient time in teaching it or in finding ways to make it available. There is also the confusion of private confession with counseling. Participants may well have other answers as to why private confession has fallen into disuse today. In this discussion, the leader will want to underscore the fact that Luther did not want the Church to reject Confession and Absolution but to reclaim it for the comfort of penitent sinners. Encourage the participants to think about the blessings and benefits of private confession. Where this gift is neglected, the vacuum is often filled with secular substitutes. While counseling and psychological therapies can be useful in making life functional, they do not provide Absolution. That is the great treasure in private confession. Here the leader may direct participants to "Individual Confession and Absolution" in *Lutheran Service Book* (pp. 292–293), pointing out that it is based on the rite in Luther's Small Catechism.

51. Luther wants to emphasize that it is Christ who forgives sin through the instrumentality of the pastor. The pastor does not represent himself but Christ. Here note the Apology of the Augsburg Confession: "Ministers act in Christ's place and do not represent their own persons, according to Luke, 'The one who hears you hears Me' (10:16)" (AP VII 47).

Forgiven!

52. The pastor is not a servant of the State (God's left hand rule) but of the Church (God's right hand rule). He hears the confession of sins that the penitent renders to God. The ear of the pastor is the tomb where those sins are buried. The pastor has no authority to render unto Caesar what belongs to God. Psalm 103 teaches us that, when God forgives our sins, He removes them and remembers them no more. Pastors are trained to forget the sins confessed to them.

53. When the devil comes to tempt us with the lie that our sins are not forgiven and that we are under God's wrath and condemnation, we go to the words of Absolution, for they are the words of One who is greater than our conscience. In Isaiah 6:1–7, Isaiah was driven to despair in the presence of God on account of his sin. The prophet was comforted by words of Absolution that touched his lips and removed his sin. Lutheran pastors will teach their people how to cling to the words of Absolution when the devil accuses tender consciences with memories of past sins and invites unstable hearts to doubt the truth of Christ's forgiveness.

Retained!

54. The Word of forgiveness in Jesus' name spoken on earth releases the sinner from his or her sin. On the other hand, the word of Law spoken to the unrepentant sinner ties or binds the sinner to his or her sins.

55. The goal of evangelical church discipline is not retribution but a profound act of love for a brother or sister whose unbelief has hardened in them impenitence. It is undertaken as a last resort and then in the prayer that the Holy Spirit might still work repentance and faith. The leader may review with the class the liturgical announcements of excommunication and restoration found in both the *Lutheran Service Book Agenda* and *Lutheran Worship Agenda*.

The Truth of Freedom in the Forgiveness of Sins

Objectives

By the power of the Holy Spirit working through God's Word, participants will (1) see how God daily and richly forgives their sins; (2) understand how God calls them to live by the forgiveness of sins in their various vocations; (3) learn how to cling to Absolution as the charter of evangelical freedom, a weapon for the fight against the devil, and a salve for the conscience inflamed by terror over past sins.

Opening Worship

O almighty and eternal God, now that You have assured us of the completion of our redemption through the resurrection of our Lord Jesus, give us the will to show forth in our lives what we profess with our lips; through Jesus Christ, Your Son, our Lord, who lives and reigns with You and the Holy Spirit, one God, now and forever (*LW,* p. 51).

Sing "Dear Christians, One and All, Rejoice" (*LSB* 556; *ELH* 378; *CW* 377; *LW* 353; *LBW* 299; *TLH* 387).

Focus

56. Our lives are hidden with Christ in God. This hiding occurs in Baptism. In Baptism, we are tucked away in Jesus' death. In Him, our future is secure because He has been raised from the dead, never to die again. We do not rely on what we see, for we still see the marks of sin in our thinking and doing. We still see the signs of death and decay in our bodies and in the world. The truth is, however, that we have been wrapped up in the righteousness of Christ and in Him we are forgiven sinners who await the consummation of our Baptism in the resurrection from the dead. The freedom that we now have by faith will be made manifest in the final liberation that will be given us on the Last Day.

Freedom From and Freedom For

57. The Jews were enslaved in Egypt under Pharaoh and in the Babylonian captivity and even as Jesus was speaking these words they were under Roman domination. Absolution declares and delivers to us the truth that Jesus' death for sin is for you. In truth, you are set free from your sins by Jesus' blood and righteousness.

58. Paul catalogues the sinful attitudes and activities from which Baptism frees us: sexual immorality, impurity, passion, evil desires, covetousness, anger, wrath, malice, slander, and obscene talk. In short, we are freed from all the practices of the old self, all the habits of hell that threaten us with bondage.

59. The passage from Colossians parallels Romans 6:1–11, where Paul makes the argument that God's free grace in Christ Jesus is not an excuse to continue in sin. Rather, in Baptism we die to sin and so are raised to walk in the newness of life. Christ died for our sins on the cross. We die to our sins in Baptism. Confession and Absolution is a concrete form of our dying and rising.

60. The life of the forgiven sinner takes on the shape of being a "little Christ" to our neighbor, to borrow Luther's imagery. Living by faith in Christ, we are now free to give ourselves in love to our neighbor.

61. To slip back into the vices of our old life is to surrender the freedom we have in Christ and revert to bondage. The freedom we have in Christ is the freedom to freely serve and love our neighbor not in order to gain something for ourselves but because we already have all things in Christ.

62. The peace of God permeates the Divine Service, giving us confidence in the work of Christ for us:

- In the Kyrie, we pray to the Lord in peace;
- In the Hymn of Praise ("Glory to God in the Highest"), we acclaim the Father as the Giver of heaven's peace on earth in Christ;
- After the sermon, the pastor blesses the congregation with "the peace of God which passes all understanding";
- In the Agnus Dei, we implore the Lamb of God to grant us peace;
- In the post-communion canticle ("Nunc Dimittis"), we sing of going in peace because God's Word has been fulfilled;

- In the second post-communion collect, we give thanks for God's pardon and peace given us in the Sacrament;
- In the Benediction, the Lord gives us His peace.

Living in the Absolution

63. The Christian life is a constant struggle beset with contradictions. The good that we desire to do, we fail to do. The evil that we abhor, we end up doing. Where will we find deliverance? Only in Christ Jesus whose death gives us the victory. Forgiveness of sins is not just the starting point of the Christian life, it is the foundation to which we must constantly return! Here the leader may point the participants to Luther's treatment of the ongoing significance of Baptism for the Christian life in Part IV of the Large Catechism, especially noting that the Christian life is a continual return to Baptism: "Repentance, therefore, is nothing other than a return and approach to Baptism" (LC IV 79).

64. This great hymn tells the whole story of the Law and the Gospel in its ten stanzas. The hymn tells of our life under Law bound by sin and death. Then Luther goes on to confess the wondrous gift of Christ's incarnation and atonement. Finally, the hymn speaks of the work of the Holy Spirit in the Gospel as He comforts us with the forgiveness of sin. The leader may wish to consult Oswald Bayer's book *Living by Faith: Justification and Sanctification*, pages 52–57, for a helpful exposition of this hymn.

Vocation

65. To forgive each other as Christ has forgiven us. Here the leader might point out that we are accustomed perhaps to apologizing to a wronged brother or sister in Christ but not to saying "Mike, I sinned against you when I got angry with you yesterday." An apology is usually followed up with something like, "Oh, don't worry about it." But a confession of sin must always be followed with an Absolution: "Joe, for Jesus' sake I forgive you your sin." Christian people should practice Confession and Absolution, not merely apology, in their life together.

66. The outcome of the words of Christ's forgiveness is praise both with lips and life as we do everything in the name of the Lord Jesus Christ, giving thanks to God the Father through Him. Forgiveness of sins frees us from fretting about ourselves, for we live under

the righteousness of Christ Jesus as justified sinners. That means we can "live toward the work and beauty He [God] would fulfill in you for Himself and others" (*LW*, p. 311).

Appendix of Lutheran Teaching

Below you will find examples of how the first Lutherans addressed the issues of Confession and Absolution. Luther and the authors of the Lutheran Confessions did not want to abandon the practice of private Confession and Absolution. Rather they wanted to filter this practice through the sieve of justification by faith alone so that private Confession and Absolution would (a) be purified from abuses; (b) be set evangelically in the context of the doctrine of repentance; and (c) serve pastorally to comfort broken sinners with the certainty of Jesus' forgiveness.

Repentance

"Now, strictly speaking, repentance consists of two parts. One part is contrition, that is, terrors striking the conscience through the knowledge of sin. The other part is faith, which is born of the Gospel [Romans 10:17] or the Absolution and believes that for Christ's sake, sins are forgiven. It comforts the conscience and delivers it from terror. Then good works are bound to follow, which are the fruit of repentance [Galatians 5:22–23]" (AC XII 3–6)

"To deliver godly consciences from these mazes of the learned persons, we have attributed these two parts to repentance: contrition and faith. If anyone desires to add a third—fruit worthy of repentance, that is, a change of the entire life and character for the better—we will not oppose it. We separate from contrition those useless and endless discussions regarding grief from loving God and from fearing punishment. We say that contrition is the true terror of the conscience, which feels that God is angry with sin and grieves that it has sinned. This contrition takes place when sins are condemned by God's Word. The sum of the preaching of the Gospel is this: to convict of sin; to offer for Christ's sake the forgiveness of sins and eternal life; and that as reborn people we should do good works. So Christ includes the sum of the Gospel when He says, 'Repentance and forgiveness of sins should be proclaimed in His name to all nations (Luke 24:47)'" (AP XII 28–31)

“Furthermore, the Power of the Keys administers and presents the Gospel through Absolution, which is the true voice of the Gospel. We also include Absolution when we speak of faith, because ‘faith comes from hearing,’ as Paul says in Romans 10:17. When the Gospel is heard and the Absolution is heard, the conscience is encouraged and receives comfort. Because God truly brings a person to life through the Word, the Keys truly forgive sins before God. According to Luke 10:16, ‘The one who hears you hears Me.’ Therefore, the voice of the one absolving must be believed no differently than we would believe a voice from heaven. Absolution can properly be called a Sacrament of repentance, as even the more learned scholastic theologians say. . . . So faith is conceived and strengthened through Absolution, through the hearing of the Gospel, through the use of the Sacraments, so that it may not give in to the terrors of sin and death while it struggles. This method of repentance is plain and clear. It increases the worth of the Power of the Keys and of the Sacraments. It illumines Christ’s benefit and teaches us to make use of Christ as Mediator and the Atoning Sacrifice.” (AP XII 39–43)

“But to this office of the Law, the New Testament immediately adds the consoling promise of grace through the Gospel. This must be believed. As Christ declares, ‘Repent and believe the gospel’ (Mark 1:15). That is, become different, act differently, and believe My promise. John the Baptist (preceding Christ) is called a preacher of repentance, but this is for the forgiveness of sins. That is, John was to accuse all and convict them of being sinners. This is so that they can know what they are before God and acknowledge that they are lost. So they can be prepared for the Lord [Mark 1:3] to receive grace and to expect and accept from Him the forgiveness of sins. This is what Christ Himself says, ‘Repentance and forgiveness of sins should be proclaimed in [My] name to all nations’ (Luke 24:47). Whenever the Law alone exercises its office, without the Gospel being added, there is nothing but death and hell, and one must despair, as Saul and Judas did [1 Samuel 31; Matthew 27:5]. St. Paul says, through sin the Law kills. [See Romans 7:10.] On the other hand, the Gospel brings consolation and forgiveness. It does so not just in one way, but through the Word and the Sacraments and the like, as we will discuss later. As Psalm 130:7 says against the dreadful captivity of sin, ‘with the LORD is . . . plentiful redemption.’” (Smalcald Articles III III 4–8)

Abuses of Confession/Absolution

"As we all know from experience, there had been no rule so burdensome as the one that forced everyone to go to Confession on pain of committing the most serious of mortal sins. That law also placed on consciences the heavy burden and torture of having to list all kinds of sin, so that no one was ever able to confess perfectly enough. The worst was that no one taught or even knew what Confession might be or what help and comfort it could give. Instead, it was turned into sheer terror and a hellish torture that one had to go through even if one detested Confession more than anything. These three oppressive things have now been lifted, and we have been granted the right to go to Confession freely, under no pressure of coercion or fear; also, we are released from the torture of needing to list all sins in detail; besides this we have the advantage of knowing how to make a beneficial use of Confession for the comfort and strengthening of our consciences." (A Brief Exhortation to Confession 1–4)

"So notice, then, that Confession, as I have often said, consists of two parts. The first is my own work and action, when I lament my sins and desire comfort and refreshment for my soul. The other part is a work that God does when He declares me free of my sin through His Word placed in the mouth of a man. It is this splendid, noble, thing that makes Confession so lovely, so comforting. It used to be that we emphasized it only as our work; all that we were then concerned about was whether our act of confession was pure and perfect in every detail. We paid no attention to the second and most necessary part of Confession, nor did we proclaim it. We acted just as if Confession were nothing but a good work by which payment was to be made to God, so that if the confession was inadequate and not exactly correct in every detail, then the Absolution would not be valid and the sin unforgiven. By this the people were driven to the point where everyone had to despair of making so pure a Confession (an obvious impossibility) and where no one could feel at ease in his conscience or have confidence in his Absolution. So they not only rendered the precious Confession useless to us but also made it a bitter burden [Matthew 23:4] causing noticeable spiritual harm and ruin." (A Brief Exhortation to Confession 15–17)

The Evangelical Use of Confession/Absolution

"Our churches teach that private Absolution should be retained in the churches, although listing all sins is not necessary for Confession. For, according to the Psalm, it is impossible. 'Who can discern his errors?' (Psalm 19:12)." (AC XI)

"The people are very carefully taught about faith in the Absolution. Before, there was profound silence about faith. Our people are taught that they should highly prize the Absolution as being God's voice and pronounced by God's command. The Power of the Keys [Matthew 16:19] is set forth in its beauty. They are reminded what great consolation it brings to anxious consciences and that God requires faith to believe such Absolution as a voice sounding from heaven [e.g., John 12:28–30]. They are taught that such faith in Christ truly obtains and receives the forgiveness of sins. Before, satisfactions were praised without restraint, but little was said about faith, Christ's merit, and the righteousness of faith. Therefore, on this point, our churches are by no means to be blamed." (AC XXV 2–5)

"Absolution, or the Power of the Keys, is an aid against sin and a consolation for a bad conscience; it is ordained by Christ in the Gospel [Matthew 16:19]. Therefore, Confession and Absolution should by no means be abolished in the Church." (SA III VIII 1)

"In issues relating to the spoken, outward Word, we must firmly hold that God grants His Spirit or grace to no one except through or with the preceding outward Word [Galatians 3:2, 5]. This protects us from the enthusiasts (i.e., souls who boast that they have the Spirit without and before the Word). . . . Actually, the papacy too is nothing but sheer enthusiasm. The pope boasts that all rights exist in the shrine of his heart. Whatever he decides and commands within his church is from the Spirit and is right, even though it is above and contrary to Scripture and the spoken Word. All this is the old devil and old serpent [Revelation 12:9] . . . We have treated this well enough elsewhere." (SA III VIII 3–6)

"How the Unlearned Should Be Taught to Confess" ‹*What is Confession?* Answer:› Confession has two parts: the one is that we confess our sins; the other is that we receive Absolution, or forgiveness, from the confessor, as from God Himself, and in no way doubt, but firmly believe that our sins are forgiven before God in heaven by this. *What sins should we confess?* ‹Answer:› Before God we should plead guilty of all sins, even of those that we do not know, as we do in the

Lord's Prayer. But before the confessor we should confess only those sins that we know and feel in our hearts. *Which are these?* ‹Answer:› Here consider your calling according to the Ten Commandments, whether you are a father, mother, son, daughter, master, mistress, a manservant or maidservant. Consider whether you have been disobedient, unfaithful, or slothful. Consider whether you have grieved anyone by words or deeds, whether you have stolen, neglected, wasted, or done other harm." (Small Catechism V)

"When I urge you to go to Confession, I am doing nothing else than urging you to be a Christian. If I have brought you to the point of being a Christian, I have thereby brought you to Confession." (A Brief Exhortation to Confession 32)

Glossary

anfechtung**.** This word was used by Luther to describe the relentless attack of the devil on the conscience as the old evil foe uses the Law in an effort to tempt Christians to unbelief and despair. There is no answer for *anfechtung* other than Absolution, which promises Christ's victory in weakness and defeat.

antinomianism. The teaching that the Law has no place in Christian proclamation or in the life of the believer. This view was championed by John Agricola at the time of the Reformation. It was rejected by both Luther and the Lutheran Confessions as it ultimately turned the Gospel into a new law.

cafeterianism. An attempt to create one's own worldview by selecting, cafeteria-style, religious or moral concepts, ideas, and practices from a variety of sources. A person who attends a Christian church on Sunday while believing in reincarnation might be viewed as a "cafeterian," for example, since bodily resurrection and reincarnation are inherently incompatible.

confession. Literally to say the same thing that God says. When we confess our sins we repeat God's evaluation of our sin.

contrition. The sorrow over sin that is created by God's Law as it breaks the heart held captive by sin. Contrition is not a self-generated regret but the work done by the Spirit as He convicts of sin.

Coram Deo**.** Before God.

Deus absconditus**.** The hidden God or God as He hides Himself.

Deus revelatus**.** The revealed God or God as He reveals Himself in Christ.

efficacy of the Word. The power of God's Word to effect or accomplish its divine purpose.

enthusiasts. A term used by Luther to refer to the radical spiritualists who believed that God came to them apart from the external instruments of Word and Sacrament.

extra nos**.** Outside of us. Used to refer to the external character of the Gospel and Sacraments.

forensic justification. God renders a verdict that declares the unrighteous righteous for the sake of Jesus' atoning work on the cross.

humanism. A broad range of philosophies that emphasize human dignity and worth and recognize a common morality based on universal, rational human nature. Humanists who deny the possibility of any supernatural involvement in human affairs are sometimes called *secular* humanists.

mysticism. While mysticism itself is a broad form of spirituality with distinct nuances, it is best characterized by the movement to transcend or move above the earthly through inward experience.

Office of the Keys. The authority that Christ has given His church to unlock from their sins those who repent and to lock those who refuse to repent to their sins.

***opinio legis*.** The "opinion of the Law" that God deals with us on the bases of our works, which must account for something in the scheme of salvation.

Penance. In Roman Catholic theology, the third sacrament, consisting of three parts: contrition, confession to the priest, and works of satisfaction.

Pietism. A post-Reformation religious movement associated with Philip Spener (1635–1705) that was characterized by a shift from the objective reality of Christ's gifts to the subjective appropriation of the Gospel and the subsequent renewal of the believer's life personally and socially.

***postmodernism*.** Refers to a cluster of themes that are somewhat interconnected in their opposition to the attempts to establish truthfulness, which characterized the period of modernity. The focus of postmodernism is characterized by pluralism and the rejection of claims to absolute truth.

***oratio, meditatio, tentatio*.** Prayer, meditation, and trial. Luther said that theologians (students of God's Word) are made by prayer, meditation, and the trial of life under the cross.

rationalism. The Enlightenment movement that saw human reason as the ultimate criterion for reality.

revelation. God's act of making His will manifest in both Law and Gospel to human beings. The instrument of God's revelation is the prophetic and apostolic Scriptures.

theology of the cross. A term gleaned from Luther's Heidelberg Disputation of 1518. Theology that is derived from the study of the humiliation, sufferings, and death of Christ.

theology of glory. Theology of mystic and scholastic speculation, which holds that true knowledge of God derives from the study of nature, which reflects God's glory. A theology of glory focuses on human reason, mysticism, or morality.